ENDANGERED ANIMALS

ASIA

by
Grace Jones

Image Credits

All images are courtesy of Shutterstock.com, unless otherwise specified. With thanks to Getty Images, Thinkstock Photo and iStockphoto.
Front Cover – San Hoyano, Signature Message, dangdumrong. 1 – Dudarev Mikhail. 4 – sruilk. 6&7 – Ivan_Sabo, gualtiero boffi, Kletr. 8&9 – Daniel Prudek, Masturawati Asari. 10&11 – MossStudio, mlorenz, Andrea Izzotti, Zhiltsov Alexandr, Eric Isselee, photomaster, 2630ben, Svetlana Foote, Destinyweddingstudio. 12&13 – Maksym Gorpenyuk, ChrisVanLennepPhoto, Travel landscapes. 14&15 – Reinhold Leitner, Nataly Reinch, Mike Dexter. 16&17 – abxyz, Quick Shot, Christian Colista. 18&19 – Glass and Nature, Dmitri Gomon, Andrea Izzotti. 20&21 – Hung Chung Chih, dangdumrong, David Franklin. 22&23 – Atthapol Saita, Tibor Duris, faisal magnet. 24&25 – Deyan Denchev, Nuamfolio, Glass and Nature. 26&27 – Tinxi, Titikul_B, Claude Huot, Jose Angel Astor Rocha, Pressmaster, ALPA PROD.

PUBLISHING

©2018
BookLife Publishing
King's Lynn
Norfolk PE30 4LS

Written by:
Grace Jones

Edited by:
John Wood

Designed by:
Drue Rintoul

CONTENTS

Page 4 **Endangered Animals**

Page 6 **Why Do Animals Become Endangered?**

Page 8 **Asia**

Page 10 **Endangered Asian Animals**

Page 12 **Asian Elephant**

Page 14 **Javan Rhinoceros**

Page 16 **Sumatran Tiger**

Page 18 **Asiatic Lion**

Page 20 **Giant Panda**

Page 22 **Red-Headed Vulture**

Page 24 **Asia in the Future**

Page 26 **How Can I Make a Difference?**

Page 28 **Find Out More**

Page 29 **Quick Quiz**

Page 30 **Glossary**

Page 32 **Index**

Words that look like this are explained in the glossary on page 30.

ENDANGERED ANIMALS

Experts estimate that there are anywhere between two million and nine million **species** living on planet Earth today, but thousands of these are in danger of dying out every single year.

What Does It Mean If a Species Is Endangered?

Any species of plant or animal that is at risk of dying out completely is said to be endangered. When all individuals of a single species die, that species has become extinct. Extinction is a real possibility for all species that are already threatened or endangered. Experts estimate that between 150 and 200 different species become extinct every day.

Dinosaurs are an example of an extinct species. They walked the Earth over 225 million years ago, and became extinct around 65 million years ago.

4

The International Union for Conservation of Nature and Natural Resources (IUCN) is the main **organisation** that records which species are in danger of extinction. The species are put into different categories, from the most to the least threatened with extinction.

IUCN'S CATEGORIES OF THREATENED ANIMALS

Category	Explanation
Extinct	Species that have no surviving members
Extinct in the Wild	Species with only surviving members in **captivity**
Critically Endangered	Species that have an extremely high risk of extinction in the wild
Endangered	Species that have a high risk of extinction in the wild
Vulnerable	Species that are likely to become endangered or critically endangered in the near future
Near Threatened	Species that are likely to become vulnerable or endangered in the near future
Least Concern	Species that fit into none of the above categories

The Javan rhinoceros has been categorised by the IUCN as 'critically endangered', with around 46-66 individuals remaining in the wild.

The IUCN's work is extremely important. Once a species has been recognised as at risk, organisations and **governments** will often take steps to protect the species and its **habitats** in order to save it from extinction. The practice of protecting or conserving a species and its habitats is called **conservation**.

5

WHY DO ANIMALS BECOME ENDANGERED?

Over the last 100 years, the human **population** of the world has grown by over 4.5 billion people. As the population has grown, the damage humans do to the **environment** and wildlife has increased too. Many experts believe that human activity is the biggest threat to animals around the world today.

HABITAT DESTRUCTION

One of the biggest threats species face is the loss of their habitats. Large areas of land are often used to build **settlements** to provide more housing, food and **natural resources** for the growing world population. This can often destroy natural habitats, which nearby wildlife need in order to survive.

Pollution

Pollution is the introduction of harmful waste to the air, water or land. Pollution threatens wildlife all over the world. For example, people drop litter, which can cut, choke or even poison animals.

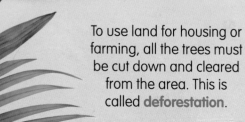

THE WORLD WIDE FUND FOR NATURE (WWF) ESTIMATES THAT BETWEEN 200 AND 2,000 SPECIES OF ANIMAL BECOME EXTINCT EVERY SINGLE YEAR.

To use land for housing or farming, all the trees must be cut down and cleared from the area. This is called **deforestation**.

Hunters and Poachers

Many species are endangered because of **hunting** or **poaching**. Humans throughout history have hunted certain species of animal, usually for their meat, fur, skin or tusks.

The dodo was a species of bird that was hunted to extinction. The last time a dodo was seen alive was in 1662.

Male African elephants are hunted by poachers for their huge tusks, which are made from a natural material called ivory and are sold for lots of money.

NATURAL CAUSES

While the most serious threats to animals are caused by humans, there are natural threats to animals too. For example, it is thought that the extinction of the dinosaurs was caused by a natural event, when a **meteorite** hit the Earth. Other species may become extinct because they are not as well **adapted** to survive in their environments as others. Experts believe that the number of species that become extinct due to human activity is around 1,000 times more than those becoming extinct through natural causes.

ASIA

Asia is one of the seven continents of the world. Continents are large areas of land that, along with five oceans, make up the Earth's surface. The other six continents are: Africa, Antarctica, Australia, Europe, North America and South America. Asia is the largest continent in the world both in population size and land mass. There are three oceans around Asia. The Pacific Ocean is to the east, the Indian Ocean to the south and the Arctic Ocean to the north.

CONTINENTS OF THE WORLD

DO YOU KNOW WHICH CONTINENT YOU LIVE IN?

ARCTIC OCEAN

ASIA

EUROPE

NORTH AMERICA

ATLANTIC OCEAN

PACIFIC OCEAN

AFRICA

PACIFIC OCEAN

SOUTH AMERICA

INDIAN OCEAN

AUSTRALIA

ANTARCTIC OCEAN

ANTARCTICA

FACTS ABOUT ASIA

FACTFILE

Population: Over 4.4 billion people.

Land Area: Over 44.5 million square kilometres (km) – it covers around 30% of Earth's total land mass.

Countries: 48

Highest Peak: Mount Everest in Nepal, which rises to 8,848 metres (m) above sea level.

Longest River: The Yangtze River in China is 6,380 km long.

Biggest Country by Area: Russia, which is over 17 million square km and is the biggest country in the world. Russia is part of both the European and Asian continents.

Mount Everest

Wildlife and Habitats

Asia is home to many different species of plant and animal found nowhere else in the world. They live in Asia's diverse habitats which include rainforest, desert, grassland and **marine** habitats.

The Sumatran tiger, like this one here, only lives on a very small part of the Asian continent.

ENDANGERED ASIAN ANIMALS

Asia is the largest and most populated continent in the world. It is also home to one of the most diverse ranges of wildlife anywhere on Earth. Because of Asia's large and growing population, many species that live on this continent are threatened by increased human activity. Various threats, including overfishing, pollution, deforestation and hunting have led to one in three of Asia's species becoming threatened or endangered.

10 ANIMALS IN DANGER IN ASIA

1

Asian Elephant

Conservation Status:
Endangered

Number:
Between 41,410–52,345 living in the wild

2

Javan Rhinoceros

Conservation Status:
Critically Endangered

Number:
Between 46–66 adults living in the wild

3

Sumatran Tiger

Conservation Status:
Critically Endangered

Number:
Between 400–700 living in the wild

4

Asiatic Lion

Conservation Status:
Endangered

Number:
Around 350 living in the wild

5

Snow Leopard

Conservation Status:
Endangered

Number:
Between 4,000–6,600 living in the wild

6

Giant Panda

Conservation Status:
Vulnerable

Number:
Between 500–1,000 adults living in the wild

7

Lar Gibbon

Conservation Status:
Endangered

Number:
Unknown

8

Chinese Pangolin

Conservation Status:
Endangered

Number:
Unknown

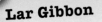

9

Red-Headed Vulture

Conservation Status:
Critically Endangered

Number:
Between 2,500–10,000 adults living in the wild

10

Bactrian Camel

Conservation Status:
Critically Endangered

Number:
Around 950 adults living in the wild

ASIAN ELEPHANT

FACTFILE

Number Living in the Wild: Between 41,410–52,345 living in the wild

IUCN Status: Endangered

Scientific Name: *Elephas maximus*

Weight: Between 2.25–5.5 tonnes

Size: Between 2–3 m tall

Life Span: Up to 60–70 years in the wild

Habitat: Grasslands, forests, rainforests and scrublands

Diet: Herbivore

Asian Elephant

Where Do They Live?

Asian elephants live in Nepal, India and some countries in Southeast Asia. Their habitats include, grasslands, rainforests, forests and scrublands.

Key

Oceans and Seas

Land

Asian Elephant Habitats

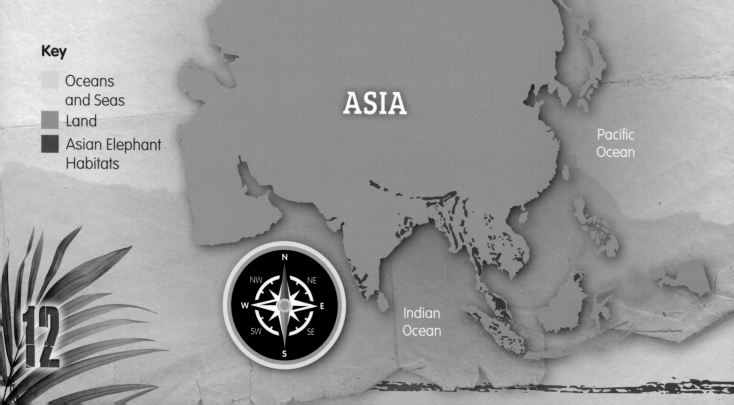

ASIA

Pacific Ocean

Indian Ocean

WHY ARE THEY IN DANGER?

The biggest threat that Asian elephants face comes from humans. Elephant herds need large territories to find the huge amounts of food that they need to survive. As the human population grows, elephants and humans are coming into more **conflict** with one another. For example, elephants often eat or trample farmers' crops. Farmers may kill the elephants for revenge and to protect their crops in the future. Hundreds of elephants are killed every single year because of human-wildlife conflicts like these.

How Are They Being Protected?

A massive challenge for conservation in Asia is resolving the human-wildlife conflicts that cause the deaths of many Asian elephants every single year. Wildlife organisations are educating local communities about the important role elephants play in helping the environment. Crops and communities are also being given better protection to reduce the number of elephants dying.

JAVAN RHINOCEROS

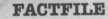

FACTFILE

Number Living in the Wild: Between 46-66 adults

IUCN Status: Critically Endangered

Scientific Name: *Rhinoceros sondaicus*

Weight: Between 900-2,300 kilograms (kg)

Size: Between 1.4-1.7 m tall

Life Span: Between 35-40 years in the wild

Habitat: Tropical rainforests usually near to water

Diet: Herbivore

Javan Rhinoceros

Where Do They Live?

Javan rhinoceroses used to live all over Southeast Asia, but now they live in tropical rainforests in Ujung Kulon on the island of Java, Indonesia.

Key

- Oceans and Seas
- Land
- Javan Rhinoceros Habitats

JAVA

Ujung Kulon

ASIA

Pacific Ocean

Indian Ocean

N NE NW W E SW SE S

Why Are They in Danger?

The biggest threat that Javan rhinoceroses face comes from poaching. Javan rhinoceroses are **illegally** hunted for their valuable horns. Their horns are illegally sold for large sums of money and are used in traditional Chinese medicine to try and treat all sorts of illnesses. However, horns are often bought as a status **symbol** to show the buyer's wealth and success.

Every year, thousands of rhinos from many different species are poached for their valuable horns.

> THERE USED TO BE ANOTHER POPULATION OF JAVAN RHINOS IN VIETNAM. IN 2010, THE LAST MEMBER OF THIS HERD WAS FOUND DEAD, WITH ITS HORNS REMOVED BY POACHERS.

HOW ARE THEY BEING PROTECTED?

The trade of Javan rhino horns and body parts has been illegal since 1975. A Rhino Protection Unit has been set up to provide anti-poaching patrols to protect the remaining members of the Ujung Kulon National Park population in Java. Remaining rhinoceroses are being moved by conservation groups to begin new herds in new areas.

Conservationists are also trying to **breed** more Javan rhinoceroses in captivity to make sure that the species does not become extinct in the future.

SUMATRAN TIGER

FACTFILE

Number Living in the Wild: Estimated to be between 400-700

IUCN Status: Critically Endangered

Scientific Name: *Panthera tigris sumatrae*

Weight: Around 90-120 kg

Size: Around 2.2-2.4 m long

Life Span: Between 15-20 years in the wild

Habitat: Sumatran tigers live in a variety of habitats in the island of Sumatra in Asia.

Diet: Carnivore

Sumatran Tiger

Where Do They Live?

Sumatran tigers live only in small areas on the Indonesian island of Sumatra in all sorts of habitats, like mountain jungles and swamp forests.

Key

Oceans and Seas

Land

Sumatran Tiger Habitats

SUMATRA

ASIA

Pacific Ocean

Indian Ocean

WHY ARE THEY IN DANGER?

The biggest threat that Sumatran tigers face comes from habitat destruction. More farming has caused deforestation to make room for farming crops and **livestock**. Most of the species now live in protected national parks. However, around a fifth of the total population still live in unprotected areas and are still at risk from further habitat destruction.

SUMATRAN TIGERS HAVE ALSO BEEN HUNTED FOR THEIR BODY PARTS. IT IS THOUGHT THAT FROM 1998 TO 2002 AT LEAST 51 TIGERS WERE KILLED BY HUMANS EVERY SINGLE YEAR.

How Are They Being Protected?

Sumatran tigers are protected in ten national parks in around 37,000 square km of their total 88,351 square km range. With under half of their land protected, the Indonesian government needs to protect all of the tigers' habitats from deforestation and poachers. In 2004, the WWF successfully campaigned to the Indonesian government to make the Tesso Nilo National Park a legally protected tiger habitat. Much more still needs to be done to protect the Sumatran tiger and its unprotected habitats if it is to be saved from future extinction.

ASIATIC LION

FACTFILE

Number Living in the Wild: Around 350

IUCN Status: Endangered

Scientific Name: *Panthera leo persica*

Weight: Between 160–265 kg

Size: Around 1.1 m tall

Life Span: Around 18–20 years in the wild

Habitat: Dry forests, savannas and deserts

Diet: Carnivore

Asiatic Lion

Where Do They Live?

Asiatic lions, or Indian lions as they are sometimes called, live mostly in dry forests, savannas and deserts in and around Gir Forest and the Girnar mountain range in south-western India.

Key

Oceans and Seas

Land

Asiatic Lion Habitats

ASIA

Pacific Ocean

Indian Ocean

Why Are They in Danger?

The Asiatic lion population was nearly hunted to extinction, but has now recovered to a few hundred members. Today, they still face threats from poachers, but their biggest threat comes from the growing Indian population. Like the Asian elephant, the Asiatic lion is coming into more conflict with humans due to the growth in farming and **urban** development. An unknown number of lions are killed every year because of human-wildlife conflicts.

Because there are so few Asiatic lions left, they are also vulnerable to unpredictable events, such as diseases or forest fires.

HOW ARE THEY BEING PROTECTED?

Five Asiatic lion habitats are currently protected within the Gir Conservation Area, which covers an area of 20,000 km. Conservation organisations are working with the government to find a location in which they can set up a new population of tigers in the Palpur-Kuno Wildlife Sanctuary in central India. Local communities will need to be moved to new homes, but great care is being taken to make sure that they are looked after and that the new lion population will be successful in the future.

GIANT PANDA

FACTFILE

Number Living in the Wild: Between 500–1,000 adults

IUCN Status: Vulnerable

Scientific Name: *Ailuropoda melanoleuca*

Weight: Up to 136 kg

Size: Between 1.2–1.5 m tall

Life Span: Between 14–20 years in the wild

Habitat: Bamboo forests

Diet: Herbivore

Giant Panda

Where Do They Live?

Giant pandas live in bamboo forests in mountainous areas of central China, in the Sichuan, Shaanxi and Gansu regions.

Key

⬜ Oceans and Seas

🟦 Land

⬛ Giant Panda Habitats

ASIA

Pacific Ocean

Indian Ocean

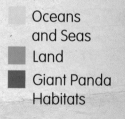

WHY ARE THEY IN DANGER?

The main threats that giant panda populations face come from the effects of habitat destruction. Because so much of the giant panda's habitat has been destroyed, the remaining 33 giant panda populations live in 20 very small and disconnected areas of bamboo forest. This makes it more difficult for them to breed and makes the small populations vulnerable to being wiped out by diseases or unpredictable events.

Bamboo Forest

IF MORE OF THEIR HABITATS ARE DESTROYED, PANDAS COULD LOSE THE BAMBOO THAT THEY NEED TO EAT IN ORDER TO SURVIVE. IT IS ESTIMATED THAT GIANT PANDAS COULD LOSE ALL OF THEIR BAMBOO HABITAT BY THE END OF THE CENTURY.

How Are They Being Protected?

Despite the fact that there are so few giant pandas living in the wild, they are showing strong signs of recovery because of the conservation efforts of the Chinese government. In 1992, the National Conservation Project for the Giant Panda and its Habitat was created and today it protects 67 nature reserves, 67% of the giant panda population and nearly 1.4 million hectares of their habitats. These conservation efforts have led to a 17% increase in population size over the last 10 years.

RED-HEADED VULTURE

FACTFILE

Number Living in the Wild: Between 2,500–10,000 adults

IUCN Status: Critically Endangered

Scientific Name: *Sarcogyps calvus*

Weight: Between 3.6–5.4 kg

Size: Between 76–84 centimetres (cm) long

Life Span: 25–30 years

Habitat: Open country, wooded hills and dry forest usually away from settlements

Diet: Carnivore

Red-Headed Vulture

Where Do They Live?

Red-headed vultures live in open country, wooded hills and dry forests in the countries of Bangladesh, Cambodia, China, India, Lao People's Democratic Republic, Myanmar, Nepal, Thailand, and Vietnam. They may be extinct in Bhutan and Malaysia, but no one knows for certain.

Key

- Oceans and Seas
- Land
- Red-Headed Vulture Habitats

ASIA

Pacific Ocean

Indian Ocean

Why Are They in Danger?

Red-headed vulture numbers have quickly declined in the past 30 years and it is believed to be because of a drug called diclofenac. Diclofenac, is sometimes used in Asia to treat livestock. When vultures eat dead animals that have had diclofenac it can cause kidney failure and then death. Studies that have taken place in India and Pakistan have suggested the drug is seriously affecting the **survival rate** of the species in every country in which it is found.

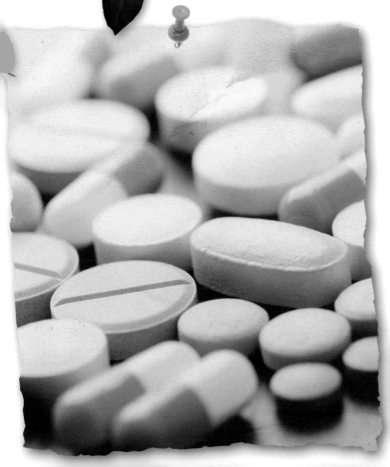

THE RED-HEADED VULTURE POPULATION IN INDIA IS ESTIMATED TO HAVE DECLINED BY 91% BETWEEN THE EARLY 1990S AND 2003.

HOW ARE THEY BEING PROTECTED?

In 2006 and 2008, India, Nepal and Pakistan passed laws that have banned using diclofenac to treat animals. These bans have reduced the number of animals with diclofenac in their bodies, but the number of animals that have already taken the drug is still high. The ban in India is believed to have increased the number of red-headed vultures there. Governments across Asia are trying to find different drugs to use instead of diclofenac to protect red-headed vultures from future extinction.

ASIA IN THE FUTURE

Many steps have already been taken to protect wildlife and conserve habitats throughout Asia, but much more can still be done to save endangered animals from extinction.

Laws and Governments

Governments have created legally protected spaces such as national parks or nature reserves throughout the continent. The giant panda has become proof around the world of how the conservation efforts of governments can save many species from extinction.

However, there are over 48 countries in Asia and they all have their own different laws and governments. Wildlife conservation programs can take a long time to become laws.

COMMUNITIES

Wildlife needs the help of local communities. In central India, conservation groups, the Indian government and local communities are working together to start a new population of Asiatic lions in the Palpur Kuno Wildlife Sanctuary.

Asiatic Lion

Education

Education is the one of the most important tools we have to help animals in danger. Education about the wildlife around us and the important part it plays within our world can often be enough to change negative attitudes. For example, conservation groups are teaching people about two endangered species that have lots of conflict with humans: the Asiatic lion and the Asian Elephant. Hopefully, education about the importance of these animals can stop the revenge killings that happen every year.

Asian elephants can be identified as they have small ears which are said to look like a map of India!

HOW CAN I MAKE A DIFFERENCE?

1 CAMPAIGN WITH AN ORGANISATION

Wildlife organisations such as the WWF and Greenpeace have helped to save many endangered species and even convince countries to change the laws through campaigning.

2 DONATE TO A CHARITY YOU BELIEVE IN

You can usually donate as little or as much as you want and most charities show you how your donations are helping to make a difference.

3 LEARN MORE ABOUT ENDANGERED SPECIES IN YOUR AREA

One of the most important ways to protect endangered species is by understanding the threats that they face. Visit a local wildlife refuge, national park or reserve or join a local wildlife organisation.

4 ADOPT AN ANIMAL

Your donation will normally go to feeding and looking after the animal that you have adopted. You'll usually get an adoption certificate and regular updates on how your animal is doing.

5 HELP TO RAISE AWARENESS BY TALKING TO OTHERS

It is important that we all talk about issues that may threaten wildlife throughout the world. By talking about these issues, it can help to make people aware of how they may be affecting wildlife and encourage them to take steps to prevent harm.

6 VOLUNTEER AT A LOCAL WILDLIFE CHARITY OR SHELTER

It is not only endangered animals who are in danger; we should help to care for all of the animals in the world.

FIND OUT MORE

To find out more about endangered species in Asia and what you can do to get involved with conservation efforts, visit:

Convention on International Trade in Endangered Species (CITES)
www.cites.org

International Union for Conservation of Nature (IUCN)
www.iucnredlist.org

Save the Rhino
www.savetherhino.org

World Wide Fund for Nature (WWF)
www.worldwildlife.org

To discover more about other endangered animals around the world take a look at more books in this series:

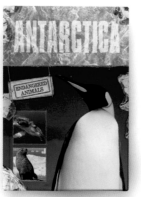

Antarctica, Endangered Animals
Grace Jones (BookLife, 2018)

North America, Endangered Animals
Grace Jones (BookLife, 2018)

Australia, Endangered Animals
Grace Jones (BookLife, 2018)

Africa, Endangered Animals
Grace Jones (BookLife, 2018)

Europe, Endangered Animals
Grace Jones (BookLife, 2018)

South America, Endangered Animals
Grace Jones (BookLife, 2018)

QUICK QUIZ

1. HOW MANY JAVAN RHINOS ARE LIVING IN THE WILD?

2. WHAT IS THE SCIENTIFIC NAME OF THE GIANT PANDA?

3. WHAT NAME IS THE ASIATIC LION ALSO KNOWN BY?

4. WHICH ISLAND DOES THE SUMATRAN TIGER LIVE ON?

5. HOW MUCH DO ASIAN ELEPHANTS WEIGH?

6. WHAT IS THE IUCN CONSERVATION STATUS OF THE RED-HEADED VULTURE?

For answers see the bottom of page 32.

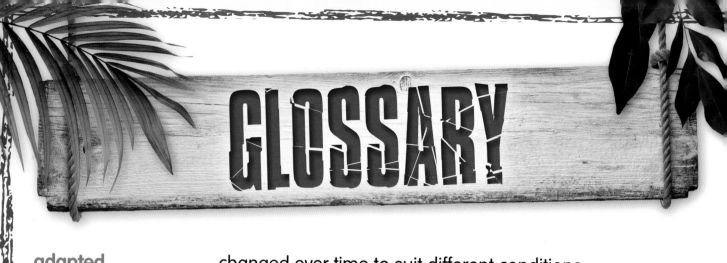

GLOSSARY

adapted	changed over time to suit different conditions
breed	the process of producing young
captivity	animals that are cared for by humans and not living in the wild
carnivore	animals that eat other animals rather than plants
conflict	active disagreement
conservation	the practice of protecting or conserving a species and its habitats
conservationists	people who act for the protection of wildlife and the environment
deforestation	the action of cutting down trees on large areas of land
environment	the natural world
habitats	the natural environments in which animals or plants live
herbivore	an animal that only eats plants
hunting	to search or chase wild animals for the purpose of catching or killing

governments	groups of people with the authority to run countries and decide their laws
illegally	in a way forbidden by law
livestock	animals that are kept for farming purposes
marine	relating to the sea
meteorite	a piece of rock that successfully enters a planet's atmosphere without being destroyed
natural resources	useful materials that are created by nature
organisation	a group of people that work together to achieve the same goals
poaching	the act of the illegal capturing or killing of wild animals
population	the number of people living in a place
savannas	flat areas of land covered with grass and with few trees
settlements	places people live permanently, like villages or towns
species	a group of very similar animals or plants that are capable of producing young together
survival rate	the percentage of members of a species that die
symbol	to stand for or represent someone or something
urban	relating to a city or town

INDEX

A

Arctic Ocean 8
Asian elephants 10, 12-13, 19, 25, 29
Asiatic lions 10, 18-19, 25, 29

B

Bactrian camels 10
bamboo 20-21
breeding 15, 21

C

China 9, 20, 22
Chinese medicine 15
Chinese pangolins 11
CITES 28
communities 13, 19, 25
conservation 5, 10-11, 13, 15, 19, 21, 24-25, 28-29
continents 8-10, 24
crops 13, 17

D

deforestation 6, 10, 17
deserts 9, 18
diclofenac 23
dinosaurs 4, 7
diseases 19, 21
drugs 23

E

education 25
extinction 4-5, 7, 15, 17, 19, 22-24

F

farmers 13
farming 6, 17, 19
fishing 10
forests 6, 9-10, 12, 14, 16-22

G

giant pandas 6, 20-21, 24, 29
Gir forest 18-19
Girnar mountain range 18
governments 5, 17, 19, 21, 23-25
grasslands 9, 12

H

habitat destruction 5-6, 9, 12, 14, 16-22, 24
horns 15
hunting 7, 10, 15, 17, 19

I

India 12, 18, 19, 22-23, 25
Indian Ocean 8, 12, 14, 16, 18, 20, 22
Indonesia 14, 16-17
IUCN 12, 14, 16, 18, 20, 22, 28
ivory 7

J

Java 14-15
Javan rhinoceros 5, 10, 14-15, 29
jungles 16

L

lar gibbons 7
laws 23-24, 26
livestock 17, 23

M

mountains 16, 18, 20

N

national parks 17, 24
Nepal 9, 12, 22-23

P

Pacific Ocean 8, 12, 14, 16, 18, 20, 22
Palpur-Kuno Wildlife Sanctuary 19, 25
poaching 7, 15, 17, 19
populations 6, 8-10, 13, 15, 17, 19, 21, 23, 25

R

rainforests 9, 12, 14
red-headed vultures 11, 22-23, 29
Rhino Protection Unit 15

S

settlements 6, 22
snow leopards 11
Southeast Asia 12, 14
Sumatra 16
Sumatran tigers 9-10, 16-17, 29

T

tusks 7

1. Between 46–66 adults living in the wild **2.** Ailuropoda melanoleuca
3. Indian lion **4.** Sumatra **5.** Between 2.25 to 5.5 tonnes **6.** Critically endangered